by L. L. Owens
illustrated by Chris Davidson

Content Consultant
M. A. Brennan
Assistant Professor, Community Development
Department of Family, Youth, and Community Sciences
University of Florida

visit us at www.abdopublishing.com

Published by Magic Wagon, a division of the ABDO Group, 8000
West 78th Street, Edina, Minnesota 55439. Copyright © 2011 by
Abdo Consulting Group, Inc. International copyrights reserved
in all countries. All rights reserved. No part of this book may
be reproduced in any form without written permission from the
publisher.

Looking Glass Library™ is a trademark and logo of Magic Wagon.

Printed in the United States of America, North Mankato, Minnesota.
012010
092010

 THIS BOOK CONTAINS AT LEAST 10% RECYCLED MATERIALS.

Text by L. L. Owens
Illustrations by Chris Davidson
Edited by Mari Kesselring
Interior layout and design by Becky Daum
Cover design by Becky Daum
Special thanks to Kenneth Atkinson, Associate Professor of Religion,
Department of Philosophy and World Religions, University of
Northern Iowa

Library of Congress Cataloging-in-Publication Data
Owens, L. L.
  Go worship / L.L. Owens ; illustrated by Chris Davidson.
      p. cm. — (Let's be social)
  Includes index.
  ISBN 978-1-60270-800-6
  1. Worship—Juvenile literature. I. Davidson, Chris, 1974- II. Title.
  BL550.O94 2011
  203—dc22
                                   2009048352

Table of Contents

What Are Places of Worship?

Churches, synagogues, temples, and mosques are all places of worship. They appear in many communities.

Places of worship are everywhere. People gather in these places to practice a religion. Each place is a special location.

Some other names for places of worship are basilica, cathedral, chapel, meetinghouse, and wat.

6

Some towns have only one place of
worship. In big cities, people have
many places to choose from.
The bigger the community,
the more different
religious beliefs can
be found.

A place of worship can be almost anywhere. It can have a building and a yard. It can be in a school. Even some hospitals have small chapels or other spaces. Tyler worships in his home.

10

The People

Most places of worship have someone who leads the group. A religious leader is in charge of a place of worship.

A few names for religious leaders are minister, pastor, priest, rabbi, and imam.

A religious leader works for the group of people who worship at a place. This group shares common beliefs. The leader talks about these beliefs. He or she speaks to and comforts the group.

A group of people at a place of worship is often called a congregation.

Some religious leaders work alone. Most have help, though. At Omar's church, Scott is the choir director. Scott is paid to direct the choir. Karen is the organist. She is a volunteer.

The Activities

Mara's place of worship is a small community. Everyone has a task. They work together toward common goals. Mara planted a tree at her place of worship.

At Seth's place of worship, services and other events make the small community strong. The group meets to talk about their beliefs. They form friendships and make decisions. They support each other. They also celebrate holidays.

Some religious holidays are Easter, Passover, and Ramadan.

At her place of worship, Amani studies a religious book. She also talks with a group about her faith. Amani and the group members learn from each other.

Sierra likes to do activities with a group from her place of worship. Her group served food at a homeless shelter. Sharing this activity made the group members closer. It also helped their surrounding community.

Not everyone goes to a place of worship. But many people still visit them. They take classes or join clubs. They listen to concerts. And they go to religious events as guests. Those events include weddings, funerals, baptisms, and bar mitzvahs. Sierra's cousin was married in a church.

People also go to places of worship for help. A singing group might need a place to perform. Someone might ask a religious leader for help.

Caleb's place of worship built a house for a family in need. His group worked together with another religious group.

Places of worship are important to many people. They bring people together. And they serve many needs in a community.

Places of Worship Project

Ask your friends about where they worship. Here are some questions you can ask:

1. What does the building look like?

2. What happens during a worship service?

3. Who attends the services?

4. Is there a religious leader?

Fun Facts

- Many places of worship study a book about their religion. Some religious books are the Bible, the Koran, and the Vedas.

- The Ulm Cathedral in Germany is one of the world's tallest churches. It is about 528 feet (161 m) tall.

- Some people go on a journey to visit a special place of worship. This is called a pilgrimage.

Glossary

faith—a belief in something.

goal—something that a person works to accomplish.

service—a religious gathering with worship and prayer.

support—to help and encourage someone.

On the Web

To learn more about places of worship, visit ABDO Group online at **www.abdopublishing.com**. Web sites about places of worship are featured on our Book Links page. These links are routinely monitored and updated to provide the most current information available.

Index